Surprise Me!

How do we get all those great ideas?

page 4

READING ACROSS TEXTS

Related Readings and Projects

page 16

Lots and Lots of Zebra Stripes

Patterns in Nature

Written and Photographed by Stephen R. Swinburne

Patterns are lines and shapes that repeat.
Some patterns are simple and some are not.

You can find patterns in

spring,

summer,

fall,

and winter.

Patterns can be circles or spots.

Patterns can be stripes or lines.

Patterns can be spirals.

Patterns can be found on the fur of animals or the feathers of a bird.

Patterns can be found on the scales of a snake or the shell of a turtle.

Some patterns show growth.

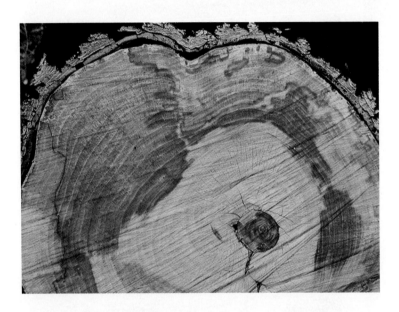

Some patterns show age.

Some patterns are straight lines.

Some patterns are
curved lines.

Some patterns last
only a short time.

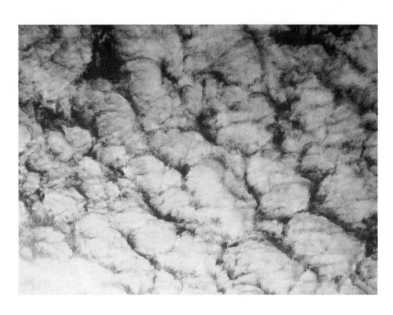

Some patterns
last forever.

You can find patterns in a park, on a pond,

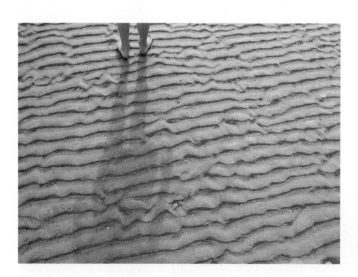 

at a beach, or on the forest floor.

Finding a pattern is fun.
Look for patterns where you live.

Pattern Puzzles

In *Lots and Lots of Zebra Stripes,* you learned about different kinds of patterns. A pattern is the way that things are put in order the same way over and over again. The patterns in a zebra's stripes are easy to see. Some patterns are hard to see. They are like puzzles. Try to solve these puzzles.

What You Do

1 Finish the pattern. Copy the addition problems below. Find the missing numbers. What patterns do you see?

$$4 + \underline{} = 6 \qquad 4 + \underline{} = 8 \qquad 4 + \underline{} = 10$$

$$4 + \underline{} = 12 \qquad 4 + \underline{} = \underline{}$$

Now solve these problems. What patterns do you see?

11	+	20	=	__
11	+	30	=	__
11	+	40	=	__
11	+	__	=	__
__	+	__	=	__

2 Copy this problem and the chart below. Write the answers. *A zebra has two ears. How many ears do two zebras have? How many ears do six zebras have?*

Zebras	Ears
1 🦓	2
2 🦓🦓	4
3 🦓🦓🦓	6
4	—
5	—
6	—

Use What You Learn

3 Make up some pattern puzzles with numbers. Share the puzzles with your classmates. Ask them to tell you what patterns they see in each puzzle.

Patterns at Your Fingertips

In *Lots and Lots of Zebra Stripes*, you learned that patterns are everywhere. Look at your fingertips. Do you see lines and circles? You might find a pattern made up of shapes like these:

Loop

Arch

Whorl

Your fingerprints are special. No one has the same pattern on his or her fingerprints as you do. Find the pattern on your fingerprints.

What You Need

stamp pad
paper towels
note cards
a hand lens
glue

What You Do

1. Press your thumb on a stamp pad. Then press your thumb on a note card.

2. Make another print of the same thumb. Look at the prints with a hand lens.

3. Ask five friends to make two prints of the same thumb. Tell them to use a different note card for each print.

4. Mix up all the note cards. Look for patterns to match each pair of fingerprints.

Use What You Learn

5. Make a chart to share with your classmates. Write the names of each fingerprint pattern on the chart.

6. Show your classmates the fingerprints. Ask them to sort the fingerprints on the pattern chart.

Starring First Grade

story by Miriam Cohen

illustrated by Lillian Hoban

"First Grade has been asked to put on a play for the school," the teacher said. "Which story should we do?"

Everybody wanted "The Three Billy Goats Gruff," especially Danny. He said, "I want to be the biggest goat that knocks off the troll's ears!"

The teacher picked Paul to be the troll, and Danny to be the biggest billy goat. She picked Sara and Margaret to be the other two goats. "We will have to make up more parts so everyone can be in the play," she said.

Anna Maria said, "We could have a little girl snowflake that dances. I'm the only one that knows how to do it, because we have snowflakes at my dancing class."

Danny said, "*No* snowflakes!" But the teacher said Anna Maria could be one.

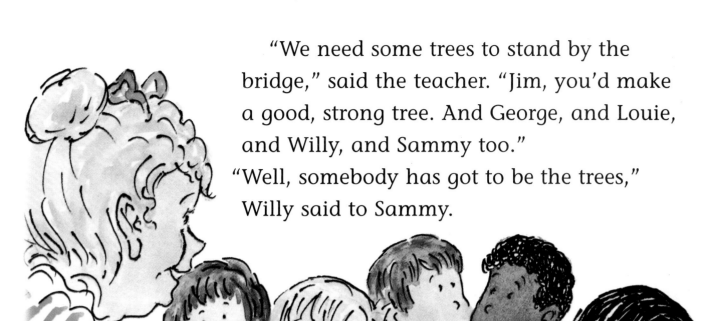

"We need some trees to stand by the bridge," said the teacher. "Jim, you'd make a good, strong tree. And George, and Louie, and Willy, and Sammy too."

"Well, somebody has got to be the trees," Willy said to Sammy.

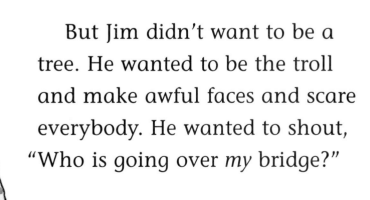

But Jim didn't want to be a tree. He wanted to be the troll and make awful faces and scare everybody. He wanted to shout, "Who is going over *my* bridge?"

They began to rehearse. Suddenly, the
tree that was Jim started singing, "This Land
Is Your Land."

"A singing tree! That's stupid," Anna
Maria said.

Paul was mad. "He's interrupting me!" he
complained.

"It's not like you to act this way, Jim," the
teacher said.

Jim didn't sing anymore, but he began telling the others what to do. And he kept telling Paul how to be the troll.

"Make him be quiet!" Paul shouted.

Finally, the teacher said, "Jim, go and sit down."

Jim began talking to himself. "I might not even be here for the play. I'll probably be going to Disney World."

Anna Maria heard him. She said, "You're just making that up."

"You don't know what my father said!" Jim shouted.

★★★★★

The teacher came over. "Jim, how would you like to be the river that goes under the troll's bridge? You could hide under this blue cloth and move around so it looks like water."

Jim stayed under the cloth and stopped bothering the other actors. But Paul was still mad at him.

After school, Paul said,
"You think you're the boss
of everybody!"

THE
3 BILLY GOATS
GRUFF
STARRING
FIRST GRADE

He didn't talk to Jim for a whole week,
not even on Friday, the day of the play.

On Friday the school band played as hard
as it could. All the classes marched in.

Soon the auditorium was full of people
waiting for the play to begin. The principal
made a long speech about the play.

Backstage, the teacher whispered, "Get
ready, First Grade. The curtain is going up in
one minute!"

Then the curtain went up. On the bright stage, the troll waited under the bridge. The trees were in their places. The snowflake twirled about near the river.

Sara started across the bridge, trip-trop, trip-trop. But Paul didn't say anything. He just stared at the lights and people.

The teacher whispered, "Who is going across my bridge?" But Paul just stared and stared. "He's got stage fright," the people said to each other. It was awful! Nobody could think what to do.

Then the river lumped up and said, "Somebody is going over your bridge, Mr. Troll. They are going trip-trop, trip-trop."

"Yes!" shouted Paul. "Somebody is going across my bridge and they better watch out! I'll eat them up!"

Then they all did their parts perfectly.

At the end, Danny caught the troll and knocked off his ears.

Everybody cheered for First Grade. Their teacher pushed Jim and Paul in front for a bow. And they grinned and grinned at each other.

Write

Would you like to put on your own play? What will you need? You will need a script, actors, costumes, and other things. A script tells the words that the actors or narrator say in a play. The narrator helps tell the story.

This is the person who is speaking.

This is what the actor is saying.

This is what the actor is doing.

Scene 4
The bedroom of the three bears.

Narrator: The three bears didn't know what to think. Could they have been robbed?

Papa Bear (in an angry voice): Somebody has been lying in my bed.

Mama Bear: Oh no! Somebody has been lying in my bed.

Baby Bear: Somebody has been lying on my bed. And she's still there! (BABY BEAR points to the bed on the stage.)

Goldilocks (in a frightened voice): Who are you?

All Three Bears: We're the Bear family! (GOLDILOCKS leaps out of the bed and runs out the door.)

Baby Bear: Who was that girl?

Mama Bear: I don't know, but I hope we never see her again.

Narrator: And they never did.

Sometimes actors wear special clothing called *costumes*. Costumes help them look like the characters.

Sometimes actors use props. Props are things that actors hold or use. The props make the play seem real.

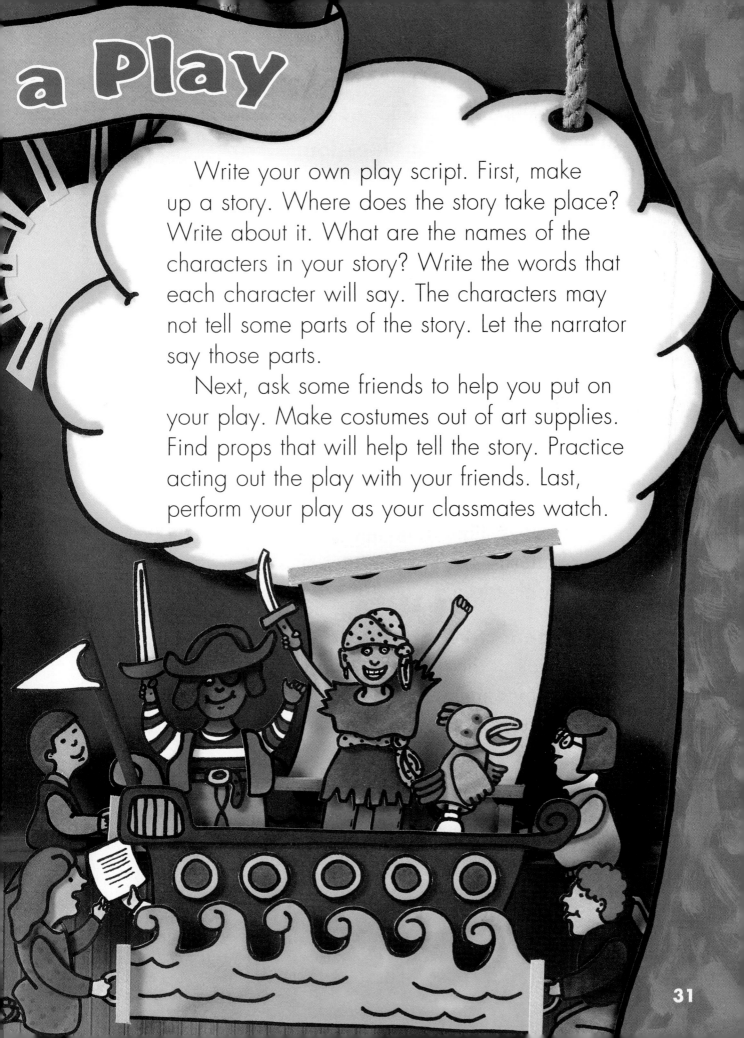

a Play

Write your own play script. First, make up a story. Where does the story take place? Write about it. What are the names of the characters in your story? Write the words that each character will say. The characters may not tell some parts of the story. Let the narrator say those parts.

Next, ask some friends to help you put on your play. Make costumes out of art supplies. Find props that will help tell the story. Practice acting out the play with your friends. Last, perform your play as your classmates watch.

Reader Response

Think About a Question

1 Where do good ideas come from? Both stories show that good ideas can come from anywhere. Where do you get good ideas? Make a list of where good ideas come from.

Ask a Question

2 The author of *Lots and Lots of Zebra Stripes* took photos of patterns in nature. Write three questions you would like to ask him about finding patterns in nature.

Use New Words

3 Look at the words in *Lots and Lots of Zebra Stripes*. Find three new words that tell about patterns. Draw a picture that shows what the words mean.

Connect What You Read

4 Look at the pictures in *Lots and Lots of Zebra Stripes* and *Starring First Grade*. How do the pictures help you understand what you read? Write your answer.

Take a Careful Look

5 How are *Lots and Lots of Zebra Stripes* and *Starring First Grade* alike? How are they different? Write your ideas.